The
St. Croix Valley
Debra Chial

Voyageur Press

St. Croix: *The* River to Watch

 When the character Mole first encountered a river in Kenneth Grahman's "Wind in the Willows," he stammered to his new friend Rat, "So—this —is—a—River!"

"*The* River," corrected the Rat.

"And you really live by the river? What a jolly life!"

"By it and with it and on it and in it," said the Rat. "It's brother and sister to me, and aunts, and company, and food and drink, and (naturally) washing. It's my world, and I don't want any other. What it hasn't got is not worth having, and what it doesn't know is not worth knowing."

Rivers are like that—they flow not only through valleys, but also through lives. People on the great coastlines may not have heard of the St. Croix River; it is not mentioned in national history books; it is not a national tourist destination. But for the folks who live in and near this valley, and for those who visit, the St. Croix is without doubt *the* River.

The St. Croix stretches for just about 154 miles (most of it along the border of Minnesota and Wisconsin), a tiny furrow on the face of a vast continent. Carved by the inexorable grind of glaciers millennia ago, the rocky limestone cliffs and gently sloping banks of the valley channel one of the nation's purest wild rivers south to the Mississippi.

In 1968, the Upper St. Croix and Namekagon rivers, north of Minnesota's Taylors Falls to their beginnings in northern Wisconsin, were protected as part of the National Wild and Scenic River system. Four years later the Lower St. Croix was added, extending the designation south of St. Croix Falls (the Wisconsin town facing Taylors Falls) to the river's confluence with the Mississippi at Prescott, Wisconsin. In all, 252 miles of river are now protected.

Much of this region is still wild. The forests of the St. Croix Valley harbor osprey, great blue heron, and many warblers; whitetail deer, beavers, raccoons, and foxes; and even an occasional black bear. Anglers troll for smallmouth bass, muskellunge, catfish, walleye, and saugers. In many of the St. Croix's rushing tributaries such as the Namekagon, Kettle, Apple, Willow, and Kinnikinnic rivers, you can set a fly for a trout.

Kayakers fly over rapids in the northern stretches of the river. Hikers explore the bedrock cliffs (or Dalles) at both Minnesota's and Wisconsin's Interstate State Parks, scrambling around the remarkable "potholes" spun by harder rocks in the soft limestone. Farther south the river widens as Lake St. Croix, and swimmers and water skiers and sailboaters cavort on steamy summer days.

The earliest known human inhabitants of the valley were Anishinabe (sometimes called Ojibway or Chippewa) and Dakota (or Sioux). They were hunter-gatherers, and reaped plentiful wild rice and game here. When the French and British voyageurs ventured into the valley, native people traded beaver pelts for money and goods. The river was food, drink—and a highway of commerce—for these native people.

Though there was plenty for all, the whites who signed treaties for Anishinabe and Dakota lands from the early to mid-1800s often cheated the native people, paying niggardly sums or not paying them at all. One bloody war in the nearby Minnesota River Valley, born of the resentment over such treatment, ended with over three hundred Dakota braves being sentenced to death; by President Lincoln's order, all but thirty-nine of them were reprieved.

In the 1830s and '40s, loggers followed the fur traders, carting their stiff saws and bringing horses, cattle, and families with them. They felled the towering virgin pine in the northern stretches of the valley, then floated the logs in such massive quantities downstream to a new mill at Marine-on-St. Croix, Minnesota, that they often jammed the river. One legendary pile-up at Taylors Falls in 1883 took fifty-seven days to clear.

If San Francisco was born of the gold rush, the St. Croix's communities were born of the log rush. Entrepreneurs such as John McKusick and Isaac Staples built sawmills in Stillwater, Minnesota, hiring daring young men to raft their boards south to St. Louis. At one time fully half of Stillwater's inhabitants were rough-and-tumble bachelors: lumberjacks and river pilots and men who worked the booms. They frequented saloons and brothels to the extent

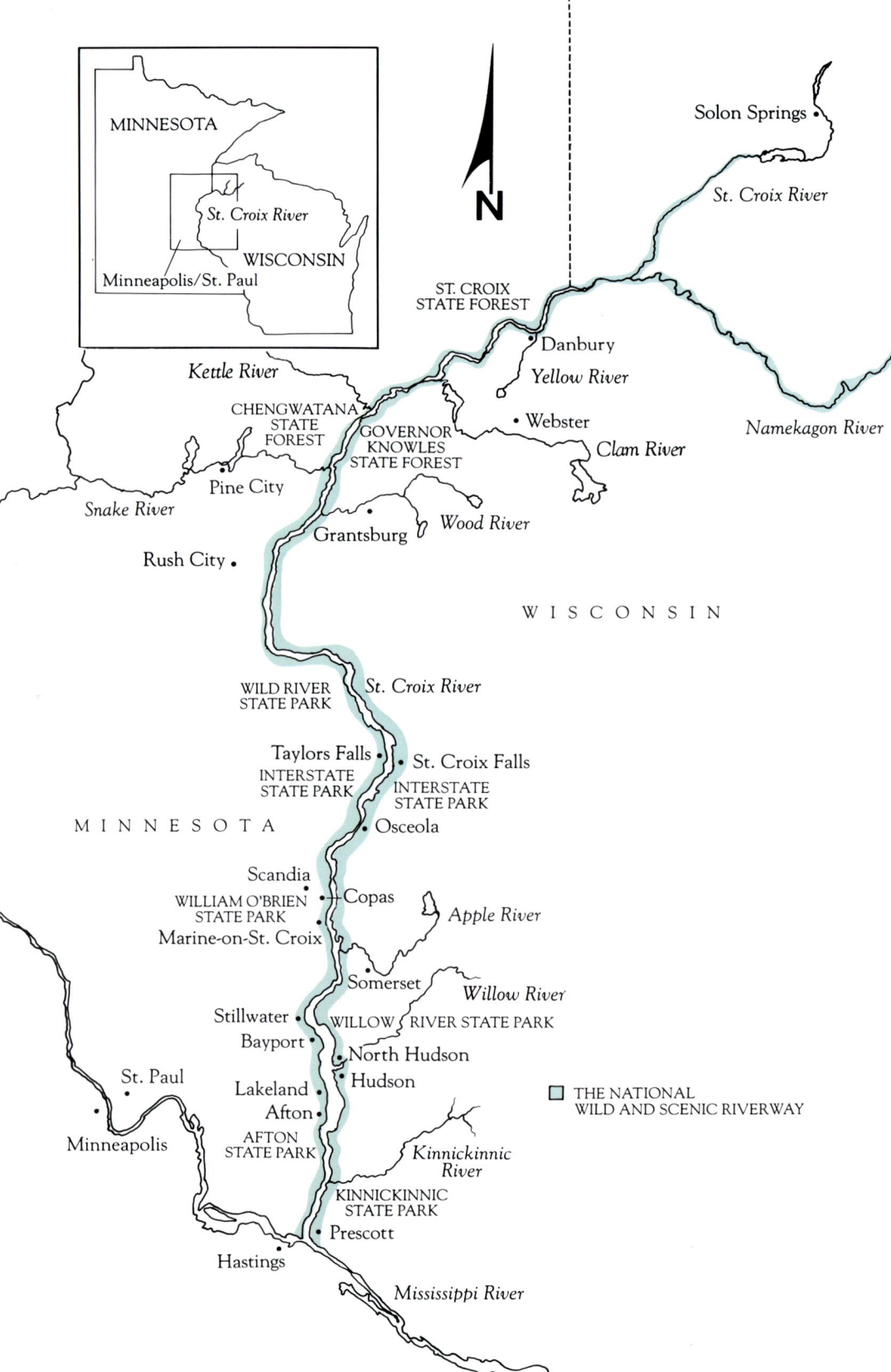

MINNESOTA

St. Croix River

WISCONSIN

Minneapolis/St. Paul

N

Solon Springs

St. Croix River

ST. CROIX
STATE FOREST

• Danbury

Yellow River

Kettle River

CHENGWATANA
STATE
FOREST

GOVERNOR
KNOWLES
STATE FOREST

• Webster

Namekagon River

Clam River

Pine City •

Snake River

Grantsburg

Wood River

Rush City •

W I S C O N S I N

WILD RIVER
STATE PARK

St. Croix River

Taylors Falls •

• St. Croix Falls

INTERSTATE
STATE PARK

INTERSTATE
STATE PARK

M I N N E S O T A

• Osceola

Scandia
•

WILLIAM O'BRIEN
STATE PARK

Copas

Apple River

Marine-on-St. Croix

• Somerset

Willow River

Stillwater •

WILLOW RIVER STATE PARK

Bayport •

• North Hudson

St. Paul
•

Lakeland

• Hudson

Minneapolis

Afton

AFTON
STATE PARK

*Kinnickinnic
River*

KINNICKINNIC
STATE PARK

□ THE NATIONAL
WILD AND SCENIC RIVERWAY

• Prescott

Hastings •

Mississippi River

that one writer called Stillwater "Minnesota's earliest whoopee-town." But the valley's logging wealth also built fine Queen Anne and Italianate houses (some of them with private ballrooms and bowling alleys), an opera house, and spired churches—historic buildings that characterize valley communities today.

By the early 1900s logging had stripped the valley bare, and the mills began to have wood shipped by rail from the north. The last log floated down the St. Croix in 1914; people drifted away, and by the 1930s Stillwater's population was half what it had been at the turn of the century.

Other pursuits occupied and sustained folks. Farms proliferated; bridges were built; and industries such as Andersen Corporation, makers of windows and doors, took the place of lumbering. Though jobs shifted away from the river, people's fascination with it hung on. Today local "river rats" still spin legends about the St. Croix. For example, they say that when city divers were brought in to survey the river bottom so that a bridge could be built at Hudson, the uninitiated divers came up shaken and white-faced. They had encountered monster catfish, and refused to go back down. Local divers had to finish the job.

Life in the St. Croix River Valley continues to evolve in some important ways. Interstate 94 and Highway 36 serve as busy conduits from Minneapolis and St. Paul, bringing an estimated half-million tourists each year. The visitors come to both Wisconsin's and Minnesota's state parks and forests, Taylors Falls's Angel Hill, Somerset's Apple River, Stillwater's stately Lowell Inn,

Stillwater's photographer John Runk captured this image of the author's great-grandfather, Jack Jewell, at Pine Island, Minnesota, in 1906. Jewell's huge load of timber is eighteen feet wide and twenty-two feet tall. (Photo credit: John Runk, collection of the author)

Afton's ski slopes, and a bevy of restaurants, bed and breakfasts, and antique shops. Valley residents also commute to the Cities to work, or slip in for shopping or a night out.

Yet the St. Croix draws many of us who live here to stay put much of the time. The vigorous cycle of seasons spins out the best entertainment. Snow wraps the river in white in winter. The rich yellow of marsh marigolds carpets wayside ditches in spring. Queen Anne's lace, wild phlox, and daisies color summer fields. And sumac flares into its cranberry reds in autumn.

In the first half of this century, the St. Croix suffered from overuse, chemical runoffs, and other pressures. Efforts since the 1960s have restored it remarkably, but of course the struggle is an ongoing one. Some endangered and threatened creatures, such as the bald eagle and timber wolf in the northern part of the valley and the bluebird in the southern part, are holding on or making a comeback. The National Park Service is anxiously guarding a pair of trumpeter swans who have nested near the mouth of the Apple River.

Though pressured by the modern world, the beauty of this stream has remained a constant. Life along the St. Croix often reminds me of a favorite haiku: "The beginning of all art: a song when planting a rice field, in the country's inmost part." That calm Oriental vision seems not so out of place here in the inmost part of our country. We paddle canoes, fish, make windows, and tell stories—all meaningful, artful gestures in the valley of *the* River.

The northern stretches of the St. Croix River and many of its northern tributaries such as the Namekagon still flow through much-wooded country and are protected as National Wild and Scenic Rivers. Here at Minnesota's St. Croix State Park, virgin pine once towered over remote Anishinabe and Dakota encampments. Now a second growth forest of aspen and conifers offers pleasant strolls for park visitors along the St. Croix and the Willard Munger State Trail.

Above: *French explorer Daniel Greysolon, Sieur du Luth, first entered the St. Croix Valley in 1680. The French and British fur traders who followed dubbed the region* la Folle Avoine *after the abundant wild rice. By about 1800, they had established fur posts at key points. Forts Folle Avoine on the Yellow River near Webster, Wisconsin, commemorates their history with replicas of the original two forts, including the one pictured here.*

Right: *Early native peoples in the valley built portable encampments like this one at Forts Folle Avoine as they followed a seasonal cycle: They harvested maple sugar in spring; gathered wild berries, bark, and fish in summer; searched out wild rice in fall; and moved to hunting grounds in winter. Some of the Anishinabe people still live along the St. Croix.*

Above right: *Dancers in jingle dresses sway at a pow wow at Forts Folle Avoine, keeping important native traditions alive. The Anishinabe were pushed into the valley in the 1500s by warring Iroquois to the east. Later, they had to give up piece after piece of land to white loggers and settlers. Many refused to leave the valley when the government tried to shepherd them onto the Lac Court Oreilles reservation in 1854.*

Right: *The beautiful Dalles at Taylors Falls and St. Croix Falls have a striking human, as well as geologic, history. Ojibway braves fought Fox warriors along the rocky cliffs near here in the late 1700s; when the Dakota joined their Fox allies they nearly routed the Ojibway. But new Ojibway forces arrived and triumphed in what may have been the valley's deadliest intertribal battle. The animosities have long been buried but the story is still told. Today carefree swimmers dive into the river's deep channel here.*

Inset: *Highway 8 crosses the St. Croix from Wisconsin into Minnesota at Taylors Falls. The river once tumbled over a series of falls here until a dam was built at the turn of the century. The community hosts several celebrations each year: Wannigan Days in June, a Log Jam Commemoration in July, and a Lighting Festival at Christmastime. The turning of leaves in fall is an equally festive occasion.*

Left inset: *This house is one of many built by settlers from New England on Angel Hill in Taylors Falls, Minnesota. The neighborhood of nineteenth century homes is on the National Register of Historic Places, and reflects the prosperity the logging industry brought—briefly—to the valley.*

*   **Left:** *Glaciers cut this channel below Taylors Falls (MN) and St. Croix Falls (WI) at perhaps the valley's most breathtaking point. Interstate State Park lies on both sides of the river here (half belongs to Minnesota, and half to Wisconsin). On the top of the limestone cliffs on the Minnesota side, visitors can stroll among remarkable "potholes," or kettles, some of them forty feet deep.*

*   **Above:** *Built by W.H.C. Folsom in 1855, Folsom House is also located in the Angel Hill neighborhood of Taylors Falls, Minnesota. An independent logger, an investor in the St. Croix Boom Company, and eventually a senator, Folsom was typical of the men who made their fortunes in the valley in the nineteenth century. Visitors can tour the house each summer and fall, and again during two weekends before Christmas.*

Above: *While Taylors Falls, Minnesota, was founded by New Englanders, Swedes settled much of the surrounding countryside. The museum village of Gammelgarden in Scandia, Minnesota, reflects their lives. Six structures, built between 1850 and 1880, include one of the oldest log churches and log parsonages in the state. Elim Lutheran Church, in the background, owns the site and offers guided tours from May through October.*

Left: *The Cascade River is one of many beautiful tributaries of the St. Croix. The Cascade Falls can be reached by descending a flight of stairs off the main street in Osceola, Wisconsin. A walking path follows the Cascade for a block or two here until it joins the St. Croix.*

Hay Lake Museum is located near Hay Lake on the Historic Corner in Scandia, Minnesota, where County Road 3 and Old Marine Trail cross. It was built as a schoolhouse by Scandia's Swedish settlers. A Hay Lake Days Festival is hosted annually here in July; guided tours are available from May through November.

Left: *The St. Croix's clear water reflects thunderheads, just before a summer storm, about a mile north of the Marine Landing in Marine-on-St. Croix, Minnesota. The river is wide and shallow at points, narrow and deep at others. In the north, sandy soil supports forests of pine, conifers, and hardwoods; in the south, richer soil allows more farming.*

Below: *Horse-drawn sleigh rides are offered every winter by Crabtree Kitchen in Copas, Minnesota. At Christmas, Santa visits a small barn behind the restaurant, where donkeys, lambs, and goats enjoy visits from small children. The restaurant is a must stop for hungry travelers along Highway 95.*

Above: *The quaint town of Marine-on-St. Croix, Minnesota, grew up around the first commercial sawmill on the St. Croix, built in 1839. The town was originally called Marine Mills after its central industry. The sawmill's company store, built in 1870, is still open as a general store. Next to it is the Village Hall, the first in Minnesota when it was built in 1888.*

Below right: *Asa Parker built his house in 1856 high on a hill over the village of Marine-on-St. Croix, Minnesota. From there he could survey a world he helped create: He was one of the founders of Marine Mills, which introduced an era that would change the valley forever. Now a bed and breakfast, the Asa Parker House is considered one of the valley's best examples of Greek revival architecture.*

Above right: *This local Indian man was photographed in 1898 at a falls in Marine-on-St. Croix. Reservations for the Ojibway of the valley had by then been created in both Minnesota and Wisconsin. However, many refused to leave the valley, forfeiting their right to reservation lands. (Photo credit: John Runk Collection, courtesy Stillwater Public Library and the Minnesota Historical Society)*

Above: *In this aerial view, the Soo Line High Bridge looks like a steel arm reaching west. And it is. The railroad and its bridges have long provided a vital link between the outside world and the valley; when local timber ran out in the early 1900s, wood was shipped by rail to keep the sawmills humming.* (Photo credit: courtesy Edwin C. Jones Jr.)

Right: *The National Park Service has cleared campsites on many islands of the St. Croix, but camping is also allowed on undeveloped islands. Visitors are encouraged to tread lightly, packing out trash and observing no wake zones. This calm stretch between the mouth of the Apple River and the St. Croix Boomsite, north of Stillwater, has a sandy shoreline; many backwaters and sloughs are most accessible by canoe.*

Left: *North of Houlton, Wisconsin, the view of Minnesota is breathtaking in fall. The forests of the St. Croix Valley harbor osprey, great blue heron, and many warblers; whitetail deer, beavers, raccoons, and foxes; and even an occasional black bear. Some endangered creatures are making a comeback: bald eagles can be seen above St. Croix Falls; the timber wolf has made a tentative reentry; the Higgins Eye Mussel is now protected by a clamming ban; and a pair of trumpeter swans has been sighted nesting near the mouth of the Apple River.*

Above: *The St. Croix is a wonderful river for canoeing. Canoeists encounter rapids in the north, but shallow water and gentle currents from Highway 70 near Grantsburg, Wisconsin, south. Outfitters rent canoes and offer return-trip transportation at many points. William O'Brien State Park is a good spot to begin; it offers a campsite especially for canoeists.*

Above inset: *Hot air balloons drift over the lazy St. Croix Valley all year long. In winter, they are launched from the frozen surface of the river and surrounding lakes. Everyone in the valley knows the sound of one of these exotic bubbles approaching: The rhythmic gasp of flames heating the air inside the balloons sounds like Darth Vader breathing.*

Above: *In the 1940s, trains like this one served passengers in the valley. Today the Minnesota Zephyr tours eight miles of woodland bluffs north of Stillwater as a dining train. Enthusiasts can also visit a train museum at Osceola.*

Right: *NSP (Northern States Power Company) was born here in the valley; the company's first power plant was located in this building. Now known as Brick Alley, it offers shops and restaurants in downtown Stillwater. NSP still runs a power plant in the valley; its stack is a landmark in Bayport, Minnesota, and can be seen for miles.*

Opposite: *Perched on the river bluffs, Stillwater is a historic community that in some ways is the focal point of the St. Croix Valley today. It was here that settlers drafted a request for territorial status for Minnesota in 1848; Congress granted the petition the following year.*

Top: *The Warden's House Museum was once the home of the warden of the state prison located in Stillwater. The prison was built in 1853, but was abandoned half a century later when a new facility was built in Bayport, Minnesota. The rocky ravine that was the site of the old prison is also remarkable in Native American history; a bloody battle between Dakota and Ojibway braves here in 1839 gave it the name "Battle Hollow."*

Center: *Built in 1878 for lumber baron Roscoe F. Hersey, this Stillwater home is replete with many original amenities, including cherry and butternut doors and trim, and leaded stained glass windows. It is a private residence.*

Bottom: *Commercial horse farms and hobby farms with their own steeds are common in the St. Croix Valley. These furry-coated horses live and play on Rivard's Horse Farm north of Stillwater.*

Several paddlewheel boats take passengers on pleasure excursions out of Stillwater and Taylors Falls. They are the last reminders of the huge steamers that once brought settlers and cargo up from the Mississippi. Here one of the boats churns past a busy marina in Stillwater. In the background is the sawmill once owned by Isaac Staples. Today it houses one of the valley's many antique shops.

Above: *A discreet flight of stairs ascends the hill at the top of Chestnut Street in Stillwater; climbers are rewarded with this glimpse of the river and the grain elevator downtown. Hidden views such as this one abound from the backyards and backroads of the valley.*

Left: *The Lowell Inn opened in 1927 on a downtown street corner in Stillwater. It may be one of the best known businesses in the valley, famous for its elegant dining and rooms. The current innkeepers, the Palmer family, purchased it in 1945.*

Right: *The Interstate Lift Bridge connects Stillwater on the Minnesota side with Houlton on the Wisconsin side, and is used by ambitious commuters who live in Wisconsin but work in the Cities. It's the only lift bridge left in Minnesota or Wisconsin, and one of the few lift bridges in the country that operates on a fixed schedule rather than on demand.*

Above: *Cowgirl Melissa Taibi rides a pony during Wild West Days in Stillwater, while members of the Jesse James Gang look on. The notorious gang never robbed a bank in the St. Croix Valley, but that doesn't stop them from enlivening the annual fall festival nowadays.*

Left above: *Church steeples rise above the trees on the hillsides of Stillwater. Also visible are many of the community's historic homes and recently remodeled library.*

Left center: *Stillwater boasted the first electric streetcars in Minnesota; Archie Parker, son of Asa Parker (one of the founders of Marine Mills), was the line's first driver. Today a replica of the original cars tours historic sites and neighborhoods.*

Left: *An annual parade during Lumberjack Days in Stillwater brings clowns, bands, politicians, and 4-H floats to town. Other Lumberjack events include dragon boat races and a log rolling demonstration.*

Above: *Fireworks explode over the St. Croix every Fourth of July in Stillwater. Lighted boats bob on the water below, and onlookers sit shoulder-to-shoulder in riverside Lowell Park to watch. Hudson also sets off fireworks, and Marine-on-St. Croix celebrates with a parade and fireworks.*

Right: *Wisconsin's Willow River is a favorite of trout anglers. This tributary joins the St. Croix just north of Hudson, where a wooded neighborhood of cozy homes is built along its banks. Here the Willow Falls cascades through one of the area's deep gorges.*

Above: *This old building in Hudson, Wisconsin, was used as a sports arena in the early 1900s. Boxing matches (which were illegal in Minnesota at one time) were held here; enthusiasts came by train from Minnesota to watch the fun. St. Croix Meadows draws crowds for its dog races today, and the Phipps Center for the Arts presents theater and concerts.*

Inset: *The Interstate Lift Bridge replaced the old wooden bridge at Stillwater; the construction crew for the new bridge posed in June 1931. (Photo credit: Stillwater Public Library and the Minnesota Historical Society)*

Looking north from Birkmose Park in Hudson, Wisconsin, it's easy to see why the river is called Lake St. Croix here. Historic Indian burial mounds are located on the top of this hill. Burial mounds were once common throughout the St. Croix Valley, but most have now been leveled by farmers.

Inset top: *Greyhounds stretch before a sprint at St. Croix Meadows in Hudson, Wisconsin. Opened in June 1991, the track hosts greyhound races all year round.*

Inset bottom: *Sailboats remain moored in the bay at Hudson, Wisconsin, throughout the summer. The owners of pontoons, houseboats, and speedboats also cruise the placid water here. The first sailboats on Lake St. Croix were rafts of logs; river pilots trying to steer their logs south to the Mississippi used blankets as sails.*

This house is host to a medley of historical facts. A Southerner built this fine Hudson home in 1857, and a local banker, Mr. Jefferson, later bought it. Jefferson's wife was the head of the Ladies Literary Society, and during the Civil War, she received mail from the front lines. The Day family purchased the house in the early 1900s. Genevieve Kline Day was the author of Hudson in the Early Days. The bed and breakfast now located here is called the Jefferson Day House.

John and Nancy Moffatt built their octagon-shaped house in 1855 when they moved to Hudson, Wisconsin, from New York, fifteen years after Hudson was founded. The home's unique architecture still intrigues visitors, who can tour the building courtesy of the St. Croix County Historical Society.

Above: *Built in 1868, a decade after Minnesota was admitted to the Union, this small building in Afton once served as a church. Missionaries, among the first whites in the area, traveled the valley to proselytize the native people. They brought religion but not justice: By the time this church was built, the Native Americans had been bilked out of their ancient homelands by a series of treacherous treaties.*

Left: *This beautiful farm is along an Afton, Minnesota, backroad—not far from where the valley's earliest farmers (John Haskell and James Norris of Afton) planted corn and potatoes in 1840.*

Like other tiny communities along the St. Croix, downtown Afton, Minnesota, has only a handful of buildings. This one was an early school. A marina, fine restaurant, and shops serve locals and tourists. Afton State Park, south of town, offers campgrounds, hiking trails, and ski slopes.

Above: *While the sandy soils of the upper St. Croix River Valley cannot sustain much farming, here near Prescott, Wisconsin, the soil is rich. Farming had come into its own by the late 1800s; in 1865, Horace Greeley wrote, "Every steamboat goes down the river with all the wheat on board she will take."*

Right: *The sun sets on a barge churning south at Hastings, Minnesota, below the confluence of the St. Croix with the Mississippi. Over two hundred fifty miles of the St. Croix and Namekagon rivers north of this point face a new day of environmental pressures, just as do all wild creatures and places.*

Designed by Helene Anderson
Introduction by Sara Saetre
Edited by Sara Saetre

Printed in Hong Kong
93 94 95 96 97 5 4 3 2 1

Library of Congress Cataloging-in-Publication Data

Chial, Debra Marie, 1964–
The St. Croix Valley / Debra Marie Chial.
p. cm.
ISBN 0-89658-183-7
1. Saint Croix River Valley (Wis. and Minn.)—Guidebooks.
I. Title. II. Title: Saint Croix Valley.
F612.S2C48   1993   92-44117
917.75'10443—dc20   CIP

Published by
VOYAGEUR PRESS, INC.
P.O. Box 338, 123 North Second Street
Stillwater, MN 55082 U.S.A.
From Minnesota and Canada 612-430-2210
Toll-free 800-888-9653

Voyageur Press books are also available at discounts for quantities for educational, fundraising, premium, or sales-promotion use. For details contact the marketing department. Please write or call for our free catalog of natural history publications.

About the Author

Debra Chial has lived in Stillwater for twenty-nine years. A freelance writer and photographer, her photos have appeared in magazines such as *Minnesota Calls*, *Minnesota Monthly*, *Friendly Exchange Magazine*, the Stillwater Chamber of Commerce's *Visitors Guide*, local newspapers, and publications nationwide. Chial owns a postcard business and sells her photographs at art shows and local galleries.

Debra Chial

Dedicated in memory of Charlotte E. Chial

Special thanks to Sue Collins and Brent Peterson for valuable help in checking facts and answering questions about the text.

Our chief written sources were James Taylor Dunn's *The St. Croix*, a highly readable history of the valley first published in 1965 and reprinted by the Minnesota Historical Society Press in 1979; and Patricia Condon Johnston's *Stillwater*, illustrated with John Runk's wonderful photographs but now unfortunately out of print.

We also drew on information supplied by the Minnesota-Wisconsin Boundary Area Commission, the Minnesota Department of Natural Resources, the National Park Service (especially the office of the St. Croix National Scenic Riverway), and the Chambers of Commerce of the communities in the valley.